Sydney Travels to Florence

A Guide for Kids

Let's Go to Italy!

First Edition

Sydney's Travel Guides for Kids
www.stgforkids.com

Email: travel@stgforkids.com

Sydney Travels to Florence

A Guide for Kids

Let's Go to Italy!

Keith Svagerko
Sydney Svagerko

Dedicated to Kids around the World

A Note from Sydney

Hi, my name is Sydney. I love to travel to new places with my mom and dad. Italy is great, and Florence is one of my favorite places in Italy. Before we went to Italy, my dad read lots of travel guides, but we could not find one just right for me. My dad and I decided to write travel guides for kids about the cities we visited in Italy. We wanted kids to know what to expect when visiting great cities such as Florence, so they will hopefully have as much fun as I had. Since my dad is a grown-up, he did most of the writing, but he could not have done it without me since I am a kid—and this is a kid's guide! I hope you have fun. I would like to hear from you. Please send me an email at Sydney@stgforkids.com and let me know what you liked best about Florence.

Ciao, Sydney

A Note from Keith

We want you to have a
great time in Florence.
Hopefully your traveling
will help you see the world
from a new point of view.
To help you prepare for
your trip to Florence, Sydney and I have written
this guide for you. This kids' guide to Florence will
help you better understand things to see and do
while visiting, and hopefully, prepare you for an
exciting adventure. We don't try to share everything
about Florence in this guide. Your grown-ups will
probably have plenty of their own travel guides and
maps and they can fill you in where we leave off. We
do share many of the sights we enjoyed plus some
extra stuff about Florence and its history! We hope
we prepare you for the amazing things you will see
and for the fun you will have! Congratulations, you
are one of few lucky kids who actually get to go to
Florence, and you will know something about it
before you arrive. Be sure to thank your grown-ups
for the trip and this guide made just for you. Have
lots of fun! Arrivederci, Keith

Table of Contents

ARRIVING: THIS IS FLORENCE FOR KIDS

A City Along the Arno River

Old bridges, large domes, leaning towers, narrow cobblestone streets, ringing bells and the birthplace of countless contributions to the modern world—this is Florence for kids! Get ready to gaze in wonder at this city along the Arno River where creativity and imaginative thinking have influenced the world for centuries. Florence is known for its historical importance in the arts, architecture, literature and science. Nestled along the banks of the Arno River, you will find this enchanting city to be mysterious, exciting and fun!

We *love* Florence for its beauty and charm, its art and its most amazing history. While we think other cities in Italy are super cool, we believe Florence is one of the neatest places in the world. We are not the only ones; more than eight million people visit Florence each year. Unlike Venice, you will not find many boats here. Instead, you will find the place where, in a unique period of history now known as the **Renaissance**, great inspiration, creativity and imagination greatly influenced the future of the world. Here, beside the Arno River, in the shadows of massive domes, you can walk along the same street plans walked by Roman soldiers. These same streets were also walked by well known writers, political figures, artists, and scientists from Florence's past including **Dante, Machiavelli, Botticelli, Michelangelo, Leonardo da Vinci, Raphael** and **Galileo**. Many influential and famous people lived here along the Arno River. Even the explorer **Amerigo Vespucci**, the person for whom America is named, was from Florence. Would you believe you can see and explore some of the same places they all enjoyed while living in Florence hundreds of years ago? You can also stop by the one important place where they were baptized and see the churches they attended as children. You really can visit history in Florence! If you don't know who these people are, don't worry—you will after reading this guide. You are going to be amazed by this small yet beautiful city and the amazing artists, scientists, architects, writers and thinkers who once called Florence home. When you walk along the winding cobblestone streets of Florence, it is like stepping into a time machine and travelling back hundreds of years ago. Get ready for time travel!

Back to the Future

Have you ever imagined going back in time? What would it be like living in a time with no telephones, televisions, video games, computers, cars, or even electricity? Five hundred years ago, when Leonardo da Vinci and Michelangelo lived in Florence, people had none of these! They did, however, have technology, just not like the technology we have today. We call people from this city Florentines, and their technologies were built and powered differently from ours in modern times. Different does not mean simple! In fact, the Florentines developed some complex technologies that enabled them to achieve some outstanding and amazing accomplishments.

One such Florentine was **Filippo Brunelleschi**, or Pippo, as his friends called him. Pippo was the genius who designed and directed the building of the huge dome of Santa Maria Fiore, the cathedral of the flowers, known simply as the "Duomo." This magnificent dome stands about 30 stories high! The building of the dome took many years to complete and required Pippo to devise and construct advanced machines made of wood, ropes and pulleys, all powered by oxen, to lift tons of material high above the ground. He was the first person to build a huge dome since Roman times. Pippo traveled to Rome to investigate and study the methods the early Romans had used to build the Pantheon.

Pippo's creative and brilliant accomplishments gave inspiration to other Florentines to develop new technologies to accomplish things. After people saw the completed dome in Florence, they had great confidence that amazing things could be achieved through new inventions and technologies. In fact, the early technologies of the Florentines inspired the development of modern day technologies.

Pippo is also recognized as the first artist to understand and explain the use of perspective in drawing. Perspective means that the picture drawn on paper, or painted on a wall, appears three dimensional and has the appearance of depth.

Another inventive Florentine you may have heard about is **Leonardo da Vinci**. Da Vinci is perhaps best known for painting the *Last Supper* and the *Mona Lisa*. However, the creative da Vinci was also a scientist and inventor. He was a multi-talented person who imagined, drew plans for, and wrote about many kinds of new ideas that would lead to inventions hundreds of years later such as the airplane, the bicycle, and a parachute.

We will share more about Leonardo da Vinci, Michelangelo, Raphael and other remarkable Florentines of the Renaissance throughout this book. We will introduce you to some of their artistic and scientific achievements, as well as how their great paintings, writings, buildings and inventions have inspired the world ever since. We think you are going to *love* Florence! It is an exciting historical adventure. So, get in your time machine and set the date to 59 B.C.; we are heading back to the beginning of this enchanting city along the Arno River—back to the founding of **Florentia** by the Romans!

The Roman City of Florentia

Florence was once called Florentia (pronounced "floor-in-TEE-uh"). It was a Roman camp for soldiers, founded around 59 B.C. as part of the growing Roman Empire. Some believe it was founded by the ruler of the Roman Empire, Caesar Augustus, himself. Caesar may have given this land as a reward to soldiers who fought for him. Florence, or **Firenze** as it is now called in Italian, has been around for more than 2,000 years. There are many different stories about how the place got its name. It may have been named in honor of a Roman general called Florinus, or it may have gotten its name because it was a city that "flourished"— to "flourish" means to do well, or prosper. Some believe it was named after flowers, and for hundreds of years the city symbol has been the lily, as depicted in the fleur-de-lis (you can see a fleur-de-lis on the title page of this guide). We don't know for sure how Florence got its name, but it has been known as Firenze by the Italians for a long, long time.

The Romans were not the first people to live here along the Arno River. This area near the river was narrow, more easily crossable and near the already well established hill town of **Fiesole**. Before the Romans, people called **Etruscans** lived in this lovely and fertile area. Today, the whole region is called **Tuscany**, after these earlier Etruscan people.

After the fall of the Roman Empire, many cities in Italy declined. People in these cities had a hard time and often struggled just to survive. The times from the fall of the Roman Empire up to the early 1300's are often referred to as the *Middle Ages,* or the *medieval* times. Some places, like Fiesole, did very well and grew during the Middle Ages, but other places did not fare so well after the fall of the empire. Some people refer to this time in history as the *Dark Ages*—but not because there was no electricity! It might be called the Dark Ages because it seems little progress was made in the quality of life for people, and little was written that survives today. Very few people knew how to read or write, and all books were written by hand.

Sometime around the year 1138, Florence became a sort of self-governing **Republic**. That means the people did not have a King or a Queen or other person telling them what laws to obey and generally how to live their lives. A Republic meant that the people of Florence had opportunities to participate in their government. Later, some people began to better understand and appreciate the idea of a democracy, where people have a greater role and voice in their government. While the people of Florence participated in their government without a King, Queen, or other ruling person, they did have wealthy and powerful families that provided leadership—often by force. Competing families fought for power for hundreds of years. It would take a long time for democracy to develop in Florence, Italy, and other parts of the world.

Like all early Roman cities, Florence was laid out along a Roman grid street plan. The center of the original town of Florentia in Roman times was located near where a triumphal arch now stands in the Republic Square. This arch was built when, for a

few years, Florence was the capital of Italy. Later, the capital moved to Rome. The Republic Square was previously the location of the market where people gathered daily. Explore this area to see if you can find some colorful horses traveling in a circular path—if you are lucky, you might even get to ride one! The Romans would have never imagined the colorful, musical carousel that rotates in the square today. Swing by for a visit and stand where Roman soldiers once camped.

As Florentia prospered, the people discovered their talents. Over time, the people of Florence became really good at working with wool and silk, and they developed a reputation for banking. Living along the Arno River was very helpful for merchants to send their things to other parts of the world. Across Europe, people trusted the Florentines with their money. In the 1200's, the Republic of Florence made a gold coin called a **Florin**. People increasingly depended on the bankers of Florence with their money, and the Florin became recognized as reliable and safe money.

One of the wealthy and powerful families in Florence during this time was the **Medici** family. Even the Pope and the Roman Catholic Church trusted the Medici bankers of Florence. Store keepers and other groups of people in Florence formed clubs called "guilds." The guilds became important in the growth, development and leadership of the city of Florence. Together with wealthy families like the Medici, the guilds provided money to artists and architects for the creation of new paintings, statues and buildings. In fact, starting around the mid 1300's, things were really beginning to change in Florence, and the Dark Ages were coming to an end. Florence entered into a new age that would impact places around the world. From the late 1200's to the late 1500's, many of the neat places we can visit and enjoy today were either started or completed. We will share more about this exciting time of history later in the book; for now, let's get this adventure started by exploring some of these neat places!

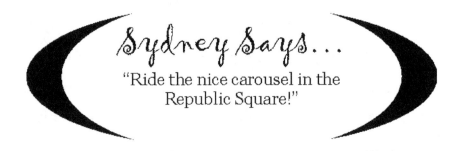

Sydney Says...
"Ride the nice carousel in the Republic Square!"

NEAT PLACES TO VISIT

Florence is home to the world famous art museum called the **Uffizi Gallery** (pronounced "oo-FEET-zee") and one of the grandest domes in the world—the **Duomo**. No trip to Florence would be complete without seeing the fabulous dome, and some of the greatest art in the whole world. The Duomo and the Uffizi Gallery are the most spectacular of all! When wandering around this charming old city, we recommend that you visit lots of neat places such as old, amazing and beautiful churches, world famous museums, and nearby Tuscan hill towns.

Sydney Says...
"The Tuscan hill towns are beautiful – get your camera ready!"

The Duomo Square

Also called the **Piazza del Duomo**, the Duomo Square connects with St. John's Square, or the **Piazza of San Giovanni**. St. John's Square is located directly in front of the Duomo cathedral. It is truly the heart of Florence and a must see location during your visit. In fact, it is almost impossible to miss! The large, red, tiled **dome** on top of the **Santa Maria Fiore Cathedral** is really quite amazing. This is the place where you will find lots of people admiring the great dome, the **Baptistery** and its famous doors, and **Giotto's Bell Tower**. If you can only go to one place in Florence, go see the Duomo and St. John's Square.

Santa Maria Fiore (Duomo) Cathedral

The Santa Maria Fiore (Saint Mary of the Flower) Cathedral is usually referred to simply as the **Duomo**. The construction of this church began in the late 1200's and was designed by **Arnolfo di Cambio**. It is the main cathedral and the spiritual center of Florence. You can see it from just about everywhere in the city! If you get lost, find the largest red dome in the sky to find your way back to the center! It took more than a hundred years to build the cathedral. Some people say the outside marble looks like striped pajamas; this marble was added in the late 1800's. When it was started in the 1200's, no one knew how it would be possible to build a dome on top of the church to cover the massive hole in the roof! No big deal—the Florentines were confident that by the time they were ready for the dome construction, someone would be able figure it out. As you now know, that someone was Filippo Brunelleschi. Pippo was way ahead of his time. He was truly genius in his drawings, designs and creations. When it came to inventing machines to help build the dome, Pippo was super smart and creative!

Sydney Says...

"Climb to the top of the Duomo for the amazing view— it is worth it!"

Climbing to the top of the dome is a neat experience. After climbing 463 steps, you can stand around the "lantern" (the top of the dome is called the lantern) and gaze out across the Arno valley and the surrounding Tuscan hills. Part of the journey includes walking around a balcony inside the church, where you can gaze up into the dome from the inside and see the neat fresco paintings by the artist **Vasari**. As you continue your journey to the top, you will get to climb steps used by the workers as they built the dome hundreds of years ago. You will also be able to see how Pippo used a "dome within a dome" in the construction. Part of the journey involves steps that run straight through the large beams that support the dome. You may hear others refer to the dome as a "cupola" or "vault," and these both describe the large circular roof. Ask your grown-ups to get a ticket and get in line to climb the Duomo; you will definitely find it to be a worthwhile adventure. It is so cool! We will tell you more later.

Giotto's Tower

The tower next to the Duomo is another great way to get a bird's eye view of the city. We really like the view of the Duomo and the Baptistery from the top of Giotto's Tower. The tower was designed by the artist and architect **Giotto**,  and it was finished after his death by other artists. If you or your grown-ups have a reason not to climb to the top of the Duomo, you might at least consider climbing the tower. The tower has fewer steps to the top, and you can enjoy a magnificent view that includes the Duomo. Beware though, those bells still chime!

The Baptistery of St. John

The Baptistery of St. John, also called the **Baptistery of San Giovanni**, or simply the Baptistery, has one of the longest histories in Florence. People have been baptized here for hundreds of years. This is where everyone was baptized in Florence. It is one of the oldest buildings in the city, and most people believed this building was once a Roman temple. It was reconstructed after the fall of the Roman Empire and has been an important part of the lives of the people of Florence ever since.

Here you will find the famous doors created by **Lorenzo Ghiberti**. We will share with you later how his creation made a great impact on Florence. Be sure to go inside to see the mosaic tiled ceiling. The ceiling is amazing! The Baptistery is  named for St. John, the **patron saint** of Florence. Sydney thought you would like to know that a "patron saint" is a special protector, or guardian of the city. Long ago, patron saints brought more fame, and people, to places.

The Signoria Square

The Signoria Square is also called the **Piazza del Signoria**. It has a remarkable history in Florence as the center of political and civic activity. Dominating the square, is the Old  Palace called the **Palazzo Vecchio**. Also, you will find the ten outdoor sculptures located in the **Loggia Lanzi**.

It was in this square that the priest **Savonarola** gained fame. Savonarola was a monk who delivered powerful sermons at the Duomo Church, and the people liked him at first. He believed Florence was heading in a wrong direction away from God. He asked people to bring all their new books, paintings, perfumes and fancy clothes and pile them high to burn. He demanded the citizens of Florence to include all the things that distracted them from

God. People threw all types of things in the fire; the artist Botticelli even threw in some of his art! The big fire became known as the "bonfire of the vanities." Savonarola became more and more critical of the Medici. For awhile, the people agreed with him and they even demanded Lorenzo the Magnificent step down from his leadership of the Republic to allow Savonarola to take over. This did not last too long though. Shortly afterwards, Savonarola was thrown out of the Church. He was burned at the stake in the same square where the bonfire of the vanities had occurred. See if you can find the sign in the square marking the location where he was burned at the stake in the year 1498 (hint: you might step on it).

While facing the Old Palace, look to the right to view a copy of the statue of the Biblical hero *David* by **Michelangelo**. The original statue of *David* was once located here but was moved to the Accademia Museum to prevent damage. In addition to damage from the weather and pollution, many years ago a person threw a bench out of a window of the Palazzo Vecchio and broke an arm off of the original statue of *David*. Fortunately, it was saved and later put back on by the artist and writer Vasari—the same man who painted the ceiling of the Duomo.

Neptune Fountain

To the far left of the statue of *David* you will find the Neptune fountain. This large white statue of Neptune is not loved by all Florentines, and some even believe it was a waste of good marble. We kind of like it and think it  fits right in! Sydney thought you might want to know why the artists forgot to put clothes on their statues. All of her friends say "eeeeeuwh" when they see our pictures from Florence. One view is that the artists were challenged to correctly show the muscles of the body. They wanted to demonstrate their knowledge and skill in correctly showing the human body. In doing this, they were doing what Greek artists had done thousands of years before. Not everyone approved of these statues without clothes, and many spoke out against them. **How many statues can you find within view of the Signoria Square?** Send an email to Sydney and let her know the number you found! Afterwards, check our website to see what other kids reported.

The Old Palace

This Old Palace is called the **Palazzo Vecchio**, and it was started in 1298. It was the main government building of the early Republic and was once the home of the Medici. The representatives were elected by the people and they were called Signoria. The Signoria would gather here in the Old Palace to conduct government affairs. Often crowds would gather here to express their political views. You will notice that the windows are really high so that rocks would not reach them from unhappy citizens! This was the place where the political writer **Machiavelli** held a government job before he wrote his now famous book about politics, called *The Prince*. It is here where a great competition was held between the artists **Leonardo da Vinci** and **Michelangelo** to paint great Florentine battle scenes on the walls. While both artists submitted large, amazing drawings, called "cartoons", and even started their paintings, unfortunately neither ever completed the scenes. Later the walls were painted over by several artists, mostly under the direction of Vasari. The Old Palace remains a government building and is now the city hall of Florence. You can go on a tour of the Old Palace for a small fee, or you can step into the courtyard for free.

Loggia dei Lanzi

A loggia (pronounced "low-juh") is a covered porch. Covered porches were popular in Italy. The **Loggia dei Lanzi** is the covered area near the front of the Old Palace. At first, this was a place for Florentines to gather to talk and  debate issues of importance, especially political issues. Later, it was turned into an outdoor sculpture area. There are many interesting statues to see in this loggia, including one by the master goldsmith **Cellini**. He created a statue of *Perseus* holding the head of Medusa—it is our favorite in the Loggia! See if you can find a statue of the artist on the Old Bridge. The loggia is a great place to relax and sketch some pictures of the statues; use the sketch pages in the back of this guide to document your visit!

Sydney Says...

"Well, the statues are really neat, but they should have clothes on!"

Santa Croce Square

In this square you will find the Santa Croce Church. This large church is the burial place for many famous Florentines. The Santa Croce square is big and has been a gathering place for public events for

many years. It is a nice place to sit and relax and write in your journal pages in the back of this guide. You can get a great view of the  square and church from the top of the Duomo and from the Piazzale Michelangelo. The Piazzale Michelangelo is a park on the other side of the Arno and we will share more about it later.

Museums

Like other great Italian cities, Florence has so many museums that it can be hard to decide which ones to visit. While the **Uffizi**, **Bargello** and **Science History** Museums were our favorites, there are several others that you might like visiting.

Uffizi Gallery

Before entering the Uffizi (pronounced "oo-FEET-zee") Gallery, walk around the courtyard and see the statues of famous people from Florence's past. These include artists, writers, scientists and explorers such as **Giotto**, **Dante**, **Machiavelli**, **Leonardo da Vinci**, **Galileo** and **Vespucci**.

The Uffizi is home to the greatest Florentine art collection in the world. When **Anna Maria Louisa**, the last living member of the Medici family, died in 1743, she gave all of the Medici family art to the city of Florence with a condition that it could never leave the city—if you want to see it, you have to visit Florence! The Uffizi was one of the museums that greatly benefitted from her donations.

Here you will find the works from Renaissance masters. The rooms in the museum are generally arranged in order from oldest paintings to newest paintings, with rooms devoted either to specific time periods or to specific artists. Our favorite room is the **Sandro Botticelli** room. Here you can see many of his fascinating, magical paintings, including the *Birth of Venus* and *Spring*. Botticelli was quite remarkable, and we think his whimsical paintings represent some of the greatest in all of Florence. We also recommend that you see the paintings by **Leonardo da Vinci**, including one of his few completed tempera on wood paintings called *The Annunciation*. Also at the Uffizi, you can see one of only three surviving panel paintings completed by **Michelangelo**. The large round painting (a "tondo") is called the *Doni Tondo – The Holy Family with St. John the Baptist*. Located outside of the various rooms, in the corridors, you will find beautiful marble sculptures. Many of these are Roman copies of Greek originals—that means they are really old! For a long time, people came to the Uffizi just to see these statues, since they are some of the finest Roman marble sculptures in the world! Don't worry about spending all day here. The museum is remarkable, but you can spend less than two hours here, and you and your grown-ups will be very happy with the visit.

Sydney Says...

"Be sure to see the paintings by Leonardo da Vinci in the Uffizi— his angel wings are so realistic!"

Before you leave, visit the café at the Uffizi for a great view of the Signoria Square as well as the Duomo. As you stand on the large balcony of the café, you are standing directly above the Loggia dei Lanzi with the cool statues! From here, you can get some nice photos or sketches looking out across the square.

Sydney Says...

"If you have an iPhone or iPad, get the Uffizi guide app to help you find your way around and see the paintings!"

Tip for Grown-ups: This is one of the greatest art museums in the world, and even if you are not a huge fan of Italian art, it is definitely worth a visit. The museum only admits a couple of hundred people at a time, and the line can get quite long. If you know you want to visit, make an online reservation, pick up your tickets at an advanced ticket desk and skip the line. If your time is limited, select a few key rooms such as the rooms for Botticelli (10-14); Leonardo (15); Michelangelo (25) and Raphael (26). You will not be disappointed.

Bargello Museum

The Bargello Museum is home to a collection of bronze and marble sculptures from many great famous artists. Here you will find **Donatello's** bronze *David*, created for **Lorenzo "the Magnificent" Medici**, and many works by **Michelangelo**. Donatello was a huge influence on later sculptors such as  Michelangelo. This is a great place to take a moment to draw some pictures in your sketch pages.

The Bargello was once a prison. Later it became the headquarters of the police. One of the neatest things about the Bargello is the courtyard. When you sit in the courtyard and look up, you see the clouds above—inside the

Bargello is an open air area surrounded by statues. We especially liked the enormous bronze canon—it is huge! In addition to many neat statues, you can find a great crowned lion by **Donatello**. In addition to sitting down to sketch, this is a nice place to take a break and quietly ponder the wonders of Florence. As you sit in the courtyard, look up at the various family crests from Florence's past.

 The Bargello is truly a National treasure for Italy and not nearly as crowded with visitors as the Uffizi Gallery. Usually, you can easily walk up at any time of the day and enter without long lines. We think you will really like this place! While it was once a prison, don't worry it is not too spooky.

Science History Museum

The Science History Museum is a super place for kids. It might just be the very best museum for kids in Florence! Located along the

Arno River next to the Uffizi Gallery, the Science History Museum has a wonderful display of interesting scientific gadgets and inventions. Here kids can view up close some of the earliest telescopes made for viewing stars and planets.

The Renaissance was a time of great discovery in the sciences, and many of the early inventions are found here. One of the great scientists from Florence we will share more about later was **Galileo Galilei.**

The Science History Museum is the place to find the coolest Galileo inventions, including many of his early hand held telescopes. There are several interesting and interactive exhibits to explore. This is great place to take notes in your journal pages at the  back of this guide. You might even write down or sketch ideas for your own experiments or inventions!

Sydney Says...

"Look for something kind of weird
in the museum that once
belonged to Galileo!"

Accademia Museum

The Accademia Museum is the place where you can find the original statue of *David*, created by **Michelangelo** around the year 1504. Michelangelo was in his mid twenties. Working from an old abandoned  piece of marble that had been sitting around for more than forty years, Michelangelo worked for three years to create the masterpiece. The statue of the Biblical hero was inspirational to Florentines when it was created and remains so today. The museum also has other statues and paintings, including the *Prisoners* by Michelangelo. Some people believe the *Prisoners* are unfinished works, while others believe that Michelangelo intended to leave them this way to show the prisoners coming out of the stone. What do you think? Send us an email!

Opera del Duomo Museum

The Duomo museum is easily missed, but should not be. Located behind the Duomo church, the museum houses many original works of art that were once spread about Florence. Many of these works have been replaced by copies. The originals have been moved to the Duomo museum to protect them from continued damage from pollution, as well as to protect them from theft or vandalism. Here you will find the original panels created by **Ghiberti** for the Baptistery doors and actual scale models of the Duomo created by **Brunelleschi**.

Also, in the Duomo Museum, you will find one of the last sculptures worked on by **Michelangelo** before he died. This sculpture, called *The Pieta*, is of Mary holding Jesus after he was taken down from the cross. Standing behind Mary is a man believed to be either Joseph of Arimathea or Nicodemus, and it is also believed to be a self portrait of Michelangelo. He worked on this difficult piece of marble late in his life, intending for it to go on his own tomb. The Pieta was completed by artists after his death. The Duomo museum preserves important works of art such for enjoyment now and in the future.

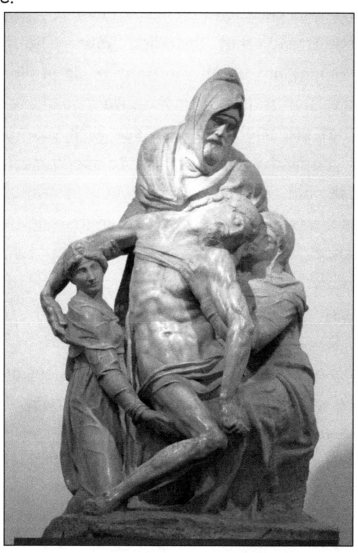

Churches

With the seat of the Roman Catholic Church in Vatican City, Italy has always been home to large beautiful churches, and Florence has many of them. We understand that spending your time in old churches may not be all you want to do in Florence, but in addition to the Duomo, we want to share a few more that you might want to see with your grown-ups. If you find it kind of hard to spend much time in these old churches, ask your grown-ups to purchase a self-guided audio tour to add to the experience and hopefully increase the fun. The remarkable churches of Florence are filled with paintings, sculptures and the tombs of famous people. Remember as you visit that most of these churches are still used for religious services and ask that you wear appropriate clothing and turn off the flash on your camera.

Santa Maria Fiore Cathedral

As we mentioned earlier, this large church is simply referred to as the **Duomo**. It is the most important in Florence and has been the spiritual  center of the city for centuries. It was started in the 12th century and took more than 100 years to complete. The dome created by Brunelleschi is definitely the highlight of the church, but peeking inside is neat too. If you climb to the top of the Dome, you will see the interior of the church and the ceiling of the Dome during the trip to the top. It is said that Florentines who stay away from Florence too long begin to have "dome-sickness" due to their love of this symbol of the city.

Santa Croce Church

If you have time, definitely visit the Santa Croce Church and take the audio tour. Here you will find the tombs of many famous Florentines,  including **Michelangelo**, **Machiavelli** and **Galileo**. The Santa Croce Church was the church Michelangelo attended as a child. We think it is one of the best churches to visit in Florence. It is both beautiful and historical. Here, you will also find the **Brunelleschi** designed *Pazzi chapel.*

Sydney Says...

"Get the audio tour and map to learn all about the tombs in Santa Croce Church!"

Tip for Grown-ups: Santa Croce is very large, and there are many highlights. We recommend an audio tour for kids. This is a church that you can easily spend a lot of time in looking around, and the audio guide helps keep it interesting.

San Lorenzo Church

The San Lorenzo church was the church attended by the Medici family. Located here is the **Medici Chapel** (the dome in the above picture). Started around 1418, the church was designed by

Brunelleschi and paid for by **Giovanni Medici**. Giovanni had started the successful Medici bank and his large donation to build the church is the first major effort by the Medici family to use their wealth for good. Giovanni's son **Cosimo de' Medici** would add much more to the funding and creation of San Lorenzo. Cosimo's grandson, Lorenzo, would continue the family's tradition by supporting many Florentine artists. There are some really neat things to see here in addition to Brunelleschi's creations, including the Medici tombs designed by Michelangelo.

When you visit San Lorenzo, get a ticket to include all the sights such as the **Medici Chapels** and the **Laurentian Library**. The Laurentian library has the most important collection of antique books in Italy. The library is really neat—be sure to ask about the chains on the library desks!

Santa Maria Novella Church

The Santa Maria Novella is located just across the street from the train station. It is a great first or last stop when traveling by train. One of the key paintings of the early Renaissance, ***The Holy Trinity***, was completed in this church by the artist **Masaccio**. His wall painting looks so three dimensional that Florentines were amazed by it. Influenced greatly by the linear perspective development of Brunelleschi, Masaccio was the first great painter of the Renaissance to use linear perspective to create depth and the appearance of three dimensional objects on a two dimensional surface, such as a wall. Masaccio's *The Holy Trinity* changed the way artists viewed drawing and painting on flat surfaces.

Other Famous Places

Pitti Palace

The Medici were not the only wealthy family in Florence during the Renaissance. There were many well-to-do families, and they were constantly in competition. One of these other families was the Pitti family. They wanted to create a really large and fabulous palace on the other side of the Arno River but ran out of money before it was complete. In fact, they went broke trying to keep up with the

Medicis! The palace the Pitti family began was later purchased by the Medici family and made even larger. Now you will find the palace to include museums. One of the very best collections of paintings by the artist **Raphael** is located in the **Palatine Gallery**. Be sure to see Raphael's *Madonna of the Chair* and the portraits of *Agnolo Doni* and *The Woman with the Veil*.

  With a ticket to the Palatine Gallery, you can also visit the Modern Art Gallery, which has paintings from the 1700's through the early 1900's. This is a really cool place. There are rooms decorated with really fancy stuff and you can read about the things in each room on a card by the room entrance. See if you can figure out the directions on each room card and explain it to your grown-ups! Located just behind the Pitti Palace is the Boboli Garden.

Ponte Vecchio – Old Bridge

There are several bridges across the Arno River, and some are quite famous. The most famous one is the **Ponte Vecchio,** or **"Old Bridge."** A lot of people visit the Old Bridge to see the shops and merchants that line its sides. Some people visit here to add a lock to a chain that hangs from the side of the bridge as a way to demonstrate their lasting love for one another—though it is now posted to be against the law! The Old Bridge is the only one that was not destroyed by the retreating German army during World War II.

Running along the top of the Old Bridge is the *Vasari Corridor.* This corridor, or hallway, was created by Vasari for the Medici family to connect the Old Palace and Uffizi with the Pitti Palace. Back

then, the Uffizi building was a collection of government offices, and in times of trouble, the Vasari Corridor provided a quick escape back home!

Sydney Says...
"Walk across the Ponte Vecchio and enjoy gelato on the other side!"

See if you can find a statue of the master goldsmith **Cellini** on the Old Bridge.

THE RENAISSANCE

Artists, scientists, writers and great thinkers; grand churches and artist workshops—this was the place to be in the 1400's! As wealth increased in Florence, families such as the Medici began giving more of their money to the arts. Along with the guilds, the Medici gave money and support to artists to create new paintings, statues and buildings. Today, we can see the amazing accomplishments in paint, marble, bronze, and buildings that were born out of this time now called the **Renaissance**. This big word is a French word that means "rebirth." What was reborn? For those who lived in Florence in the early 1400's, the way of thinking about art, science and life was reborn. This rebirth changed perceptions about life and beauty. The people of Florence have inherited much from the Renaissance.

The Renaissance was a rebirth of classical ideals. People wanted to learn and gain a greater understanding of the Greek and Roman cultures that had disappeared hundreds of years before their own time. Greek writings such as those by Plato and Aristotle were translated into Italian. People like **Leonardo da Vinci** were amazed by the thinking and logic of Plato and Aristotle.

While the Renaissance came to life in the 1400's, there was a period of about three hundred years ranging from around 1350 to around 1650 now considered the "early" to the "high" Renaissance. We will focus mostly on the early Renaissance and how art and science came alive in Florence! This was an exciting period of amazing progress and set the stage for even greater progress in the arts and sciences. The Renaissance was a time of creativity and the making of new things. It was a time described by a famous author named Voltaire as one of the greatest times in world history.

People don't agree about when the Renaissance started and ended. We know that in 1401 there was a competition to create large bronze doors for the Baptistery of St. John. Since the Baptistery was so loved by Florentines, people recognized it was a very important competition. Some believe the competition was a turning point in the history of the city. Seven people entered the competition, and the finalists were **Lorenzo Ghiberti** and **Filippo Brunelleschi**. Both of these Florentines were young men, and both very much wanted to be chosen to create the doors. In the competition, they were asked to design a bronze panel showing the sacrifice of Isaac, as told in the Old Testament of the Holy Bible. While both were very excellent, the judges chose the work of Ghiberti. He worked on the doors for more than 20 years before completing them! This was important— since Brunelleschi did not win the door competition, he focused his efforts on being chosen to design and build the great dome for the Duomo church.

Both men achieved great and lasting contributions to Florence. Lorenzo Ghiberti's three dimensional bronze panels, showing different scenes from the Old Testament, have been called the most beautiful doors ever created—people loved them then and still do! You can now see the original bronze panels in the Opera del Duomo Museum. When Michelangelo saw the doors created by Ghiberti he said they were so beautiful they could be the gates of Heaven.

Brunelleschi's triumph in completing the dome for the cathedral showed the ability of people to overcome tremendous obstacles. People started thinking,  "Wow, we can accomplish great things!" Some people think the completion of the large dome and the bronze doors of the baptistery were the true beginning of the Renaissance. While there is no official start and end date, the 1400's and early 1500's were a time of great optimism in Florence and in other parts of the world. In fact, in 1492, a man named Christopher Columbus "sailed the ocean blue."

Amazing Artists of the Renaissance

Artists were not always viewed as special. For much of history, artists were seen as craftsmen simply following instructions in their creations, as other trades that worked with their hands. This all began to change during the Renaissance, and part of the reason is the rise of the "patron". Do you know what a patron is? A patron is someone who gives money to support something or someone. During the Renaissance, artists needed patrons so they could focus on their creative talents and not have to worry about earning money for food and shelter. One of the most influential patron families in Florence was the Medici. During this time, art was a great luxury. Historically, only the church had asked artists to paint pictures. Now, with increasing wealth, families were hiring artists to paint pictures and create statues. Art was changing and becoming more about creating pictures and sculptures for people's enjoyment.

Leading Florence out of the Middle Ages was the artist **Giotto**. He is recognized for greater realism in painting and influenced the development of the Renaissance in Florence. Following Giotto, Donatello, was born in 1386. **Donatello** was an early Renaissance artist and is known for his bronze sculptures. He was a friend of **Cosimo de Medici** and was an apprentice to Lorenzo Ghiberti. Donatello's sculptures greatly influenced later sculptors like **Michelangelo.** Many of their famous works of art are now in the **Bargello Museum**. The early workshops of **Ghirlandaio** and **Verrocchio** significantly influenced generations of fresco painters such as **Leonardo da Vinci, Botticelli, Michelangelo** and **Raphael.**

Leonardo da Vinci

At about the age of fourteen, **Leonardo da Vinci** became an apprentice in the workshop of **Verrocchio**. This was an honor, for Verrocchio was a master painter with **Lorenzo Medici** as a patron. After completing his apprenticeship and working on his own for a few years, da Vinci decided to leave Florence when he was about 30 years old.

He went to Milan to work for the Duke of Milan as a member of the Duke's court. While there he completed six paintings in seventeen years. One of his major works completed in Milan is *The Last Supper*, depicting Jesus Christ with his twelve disciples. Da Vinci was magnificent at capturing the emotions in their faces when Jesus told them that one of them would betray him. Unfortunately, da Vinci experimented with the paints and process he used to create *The Last Supper* and it began to deteriorate shortly after he completed it. When the Duke of Milan lost power to the French, da Vinci left and made his way back to Florence. In 1503 he began painting the *Mona Lisa*. Da Vinci worked on the *Mona Lisa* for most of the rest of his life, completing it just before he died in France in 1519. The location where he was buried in France was lost and remains unknown.

Sandro Botticelli

One of our favorite painters of the Renaissance is Sandro Botticelli. Many of his paintings are in the **Uffizi Gallery**. Botticelli apprenticed in **Verrocchio's workshop**. Botticelli departed from his fellow painters in the many ways. Several of his paintings included figures from Greek myths. His mythical paintings, such as ***The Birth of Venus*** and ***Spring***, are highly creative and fun natured. We think his round paintings, called tondos, are some of the most beautiful paintings ever created—our favorite tondo in the Uffizi is the ***Madonna of the Magnificat***.

Michelangelo

Michelangelo Buonarroti was
born in 1475. As a young boy
he learned about creating
things with a hammer and a
chisel. He was apprenticed to
the famous master painter
Ghirlandaio. Michelangelo was
a great sculptor and painter
who left a tremendous legacy
of beauty in his marble

creations found throughout Italy. Over several
years he created the amazing fresco paintings on
the ceiling of the Sistine Chapel in Rome. A fresco is
a painting done on walls or ceilings where the paint is
applied in fresh plaster and becomes part of the wall
or ceiling when the plaster dries. In Florence his
most famous sculpture is the statue of *David* which
is now located in the **Accademia Museum**. Other
sculptural works in Florence include *The Pieta* in the
Duomo Museum, *Bacchus* in the **Bargello Museum**,

and one of his few paintings on wood, the *Doni Tondo - The Holy Family with St. John the Baptist,* in the **Uffizi Gallery**. His sculptures of *Figure of Day* and *Figure of Night* are found on a Medici tomb in **Medici Chapel** at San Lorenzo. He died in Rome in 1564, and his tomb is located in Santa Croce Church.

Raphael

Born in 1483, Raphael quickly rose in fame and popularity. He was recognized quickly as a very talented artist with life like drawings and paintings. He respected and studied the works of da Vinci and Michelangelo, and while he died at the young age of 37, he left a great contribution to the world in his beautiful paintings. Many of his paintings are located in the Pitti Palace. See his *Madonna of the Goldfinch* and *Leo X and Cardinals* in the **Uffizi Gallery**. Other highlights of Raphael's short career include the frescos he completed on the walls of the Pope's apartments in The Vatican. These include The *Liberation of St. Peter* and *The School of Athens.*

For the largest collection of Raphael paintings in Florence, visit the **Pitti Palace** and be sure to see *Madonna of the Chair* and the portraits of *Agnolo Doni* and *The Woman with the Veil*.

Masaccio

The joining of art and mathematics resulted in more realistic looking drawings and paintings. While Brunelleschi developed the ideas of linear perspective in drawing, Masaccio was one of the first painters in Florence to make paintings look more three dimensional and less flat. He painted early in the Renaissance in the Santa Maria Novella Church, and his masterpiece *The Holy Trinity* is located there today. See if you can find this picture that so influenced many later artists in the ideas of linear perspective.

Vasari

In addition to repairing the arm of Michelangelo's *David* and painting the ceiling of the Duomo, Vasari is known for his book *The Lives of the Artists*. While not as well known as so many of the famous artists we have highlighted in this guide, we owe much to Vasari for our modern understanding of Renaissance artists. In addition to his important writings about Florentine artists, Vasari was an artist himself and a big fan of Michelangelo. He created the tomb for Michelangelo in Santa Croce Church. Recall that he also created the corridor linking the Old Palace with the Pitti Palace along the top of the Old Bridge. He is also known for painting the ceilings in the Palazzo Vecchio. Vasari may not be as well recognized as other masters of the Renaissance, but we think he made some pretty lasting contributions to Florence!

Amazing Scientists of the Renaissance

In addition to progress in art, the Renaissance was a time of pursuit of knowledge in science and math. While many contributed to scientific advances in Italy and other parts of Europe, we will focus on the Florentines **Paolo Toscanelli, Leonardo da Vinci** and **Galileo Galilei.**

Paolo Toscanelli

The Florentine **Paolo Toscanelli**, born in 1397, was a well known mathematician and astronomer. He spent hours upon hours observing the night sky to track and record the movement of comets. He observed and tracked what would later be called *Halley's Comet* (named after the person who verified its return). He assisted his good friend Brunelleschi in building an astronomical instrument in the Duomo. The instrument measured the exact position of the sun during the summer to identify important times such as the appropriate time to plant seeds and the time to harvest. Toscanelli made some very accurate measurements with the device. **Christopher Columbus** may have received a letter and map from Toscanelli that provided him with important information and ideas to support the view of traveling west by sea to reach the Far East. Toscanelli's ideas and writings influenced many Florentine scientists of the Renaissance, including Leonardo da Vinci.

Leonardo da Vinci

By now, you may have come to realize that da Vinci was a great example of a "Renaissance Man" as we think of one today. In addition to being an artist, da Vinci was an inventor and scientist. He was always questioning things and wanted to know how things worked in the world. He was fascinated with the human body and how it functions, particularly the eyes and the circulation of blood. He spent many hours studying human skeletal and muscular systems through dissections. As an artist, he created some of the most detailed drawings of the human ever made. These drawings greatly assisted the developing medical profession. Throughout his life da Vinci wrote about his ideas, and sketched drawings in notebooks that he carried around with him. In these notebooks, da Vinci developed his ideas regarding his scientific experiments and potential inventions. He carried a notebook with him wherever he went.

Da Vinci was especially fascinated with flight and studied birds extensively. Many of his paintings that included angels show his attention to the details of a bird's feathers and wings. He wanted to develop a way for humans to fly and he may have made attempts with some of his experiments. He drew designs for a parachute long before we know of one being developed. It seems his primary limit as an inventor was the lack of materials he had to work with. Many of da Vinci's notebooks have survived to this day. Did you know that all of the writings in Leonardo da Vinci's notebooks were written in reverse? You need a mirror to read them!

Galileo Galilei

One of the most celebrated astronomers of Florence in the late Renaissance was Galileo Galilei. Galileo was born in the year that Michelangelo died—1564. Four hundred years ago in 1610, during the high Renaissance, Galileo pointed his telescope to

the sky and discovered that Jupiter has orbiting moons! His discovery was the first to show evidence that something orbited a body in space other than the Earth. Up to that time, people believed that Earth was the center of the Universe. People were amazed and in disbelief! Most people thought he was wrong, but he was not. His discovery created quite an uproar, especially in his church. Galileo was a religious man and believed that his discoveries were not in conflict with religious teachings. His work would greatly influence the coming scientific revolution throughout Europe. Visit the Science Museum to learn more about his ideas, instruments, experiments and discoveries.

Other Amazing People of the Renaissance

In addition to the great artists and scientists we have shared with you, we would like to share a little more about some amazing people from Florence.

Cosimo de' Medici

Following in his father Giovanni's footsteps, Cosimo became a great patron of the arts. During his life he earned great sums of money in banking. Because charging interest on loans was considered bad behavior, Cosimo seemed to make a great effort to give lots of money to churches such as San Lorenzo. His grandson Lorenzo became an even greater patron of the arts.

Lorenzo "The Magnificent" Medici

Lorenzo was an excellent politician and well educated. He had a circle of intellectual friends and spent much time discussing the newly translated Greek classical books. He inherited Cosimo's rare book collection and had the best private library in

Florence. Books were handmade, very expensive and hard to find. There were no public libraries!

Lorenzo was very interested in the arts and financially supported **Verrocchio**, the master who apprenticed **Leonardo da Vinci** and **Botticelli**. He also supported the young **Michelangelo**. Lorenzo started a sculpture school at San Marco to advance talented sculptors such as Michelangelo. His patronage brought the Renaissance to a peak in Florence. When he died young in 1492, many believed the city and the Renaissance began a decline, or at least moved to other parts of Italy such as Rome.

Dante Alighieri

Some consider Dante the father of the Italian language. Born in Florence in 1265, he was the first author to write in the language of the locals and not in Latin. His famous book is called *The Divine Comedy* written in the early 1300's, the earliest years of the Renaissance. *The Divine Comedy* made a significant impact on people and continues to be one of the most important books ever written.

Machiavelli

Niccolo Machiavelli, another famous Florentine author, is known for his political writings. He held a government position in Florence and was well respected until those who held power changed. He was accused as a traitor, tortured and then jailed. When he was released, he left Florence and wrote a book in 1513 called *The Prince*. The book, about how leaders should rule others, is debated even today.

Amerigo Vespucci

Following in the direction of the 1492 journey of Christopher Columbus, **Amerigo Vespucci** was an explorer who made sea voyages around 1500. When he returned to Florence he wrote letters about his journey and the places he visited. Most people were generally unfamiliar with these new places and some map makers identified these areas with Amerigo, eventually leading to the naming of "America." Amerigo was friends with Leonardo da Vinci.

VISITING TUSCAN HILL TOWNS

If you have time to visit some of the beautiful and historical Tuscan hill towns surrounding Florence, we recommend several. The closest one to visit from Florence is **Fiesole.** This old town can be reached by bus and sits above the Arno valley with a great view of Florence. Fiesole was founded well before Florence and remains a vibrant town with interesting ruins from Etruscan and Roman times.

Lucca

If you would like to go for a nice bike ride, then we recommend traveling to the hill town of Lucca. This is a nice quiet place to relax. You and your grown-ups can rent bikes here at several locations along the city rampart. A rampart is kind of like a city wall, but much wider. The rampart in Lucca is a wide path more than two miles long circling the old town. This beautiful tree lined path is slightly elevated and provides a nice view of the old town on a bike or by foot. You can even rent a double seated two person bike! While visiting we recommend lunch at the old roman amphitheater. There you will find cafés with outdoor seating around the circular area. It is hard to visit Tuscan hill towns without venturing out to see the famous town of Pisa located not far from Lucca.

Pisa

In Pisa you will find the "Field of Miracles" and the world famous **Leaning Tower of Pisa**. Join in the fun and have someone take your picture "holding the leaning tower up" (this is accomplished by holding your hands in a line along the distant tower in the  background). If time permits, purchase tickets to walk up to the top of the leaning tower. We really enjoyed visiting the large cathedral next to the leaning tower. We felt so welcomed by the staff and they told us that unlike the large churches in Florence, we were welcome to take as many flash photos as we liked! Sydney enjoyed making donations to light candles for loved ones.

Tip for Grown-ups: From the parking lot to the entrance, be prepared for potentially eager street vendors persistently selling their goods. Inside the area near the cathedral are vendors offering souvenirs more in line with what you might expect.

Sydney Says...

"Be sure have your petting hand ready— Pisa is a great place to meet Italian pets!"

San Gimagnano

South of Florence you will find one of the coolest hill towns in Tuscany, called San Gimignano. We love this neat hill top town with its tall towers reaching into the sky. Once upon a time there were many more towers—an early version of "skyscrapers" long before modern day buildings. Just about every family had one! You will find many small outdoor squares with lovely music filling the air. This is a great place to enjoy a meal. With its hill top location, we think it is a great place for photos of the Tuscan landscape before sunset. If you are shopping for gifts and souvenirs, San Gimagnano has a great selection of Italian ceramics. This small town has all the charm you would hope to find in Tuscany.

Siena

Wow! Next to long time rival Florence, Siena might just be the coolest Tuscan hill town to visit. Like Florence, Siena was an independent city-state for hundreds of years. It has a much different feel than Florence. Siena is known for its famous medieval horse race called the Palio, held  twice each year. We highly recommend that you visit **Piazza Del Campo** and the Cathedral of Siena. **The Piazza Del Campo** is the main city square and is a nice place to sketch pictures and take photographs. We recommend lunch in the square with an after desert walk to the Cathedral.

PARKS

If you get a little tired of being indoors, you can rest your feet in one of Florence's scenic parks. One nice place to relax, write in your journal or sketch pictures is in the Boboli Gardens, another is in Piazzale Michelangelo.

Boboli Gardens

The Boboli Gardens are located directly behind the Pitti Palace in the Oltrarno, or other side of the Arno River. This is one of the most peaceful places to relax and enjoy the lush landscaping and water fountains. The park is huge, with statues, fountains and plants. While not free, it is part of a combination ticket to see some minor museums at the Pitti Palace, such as the Silver Museum. The Boboli Gardens are located just behind the Pitti Palace and near Fort Belvedere. If you make it to Boboli Gardens, definitely travel a little further for one of the best views in Florence at Piazzale Michelangelo.

Piazzale Michelangelo

Piazzale Michelangelo is an awesome place to visit. It is definitely one of the top places to see in Florence. When you stand across the Arno River at the Piazzale Michelangelo, you can enjoy picture perfect views. In fact, many of the pictures you might see of Florence are taken from this location! This is a great place to sketch a drawing on the sketch pages included in the back of this guide. While you sketch, your grown-ups can take lots of photographs and simply enjoy the views. If you have a camera, this would be an excellent time to use it!

If you are walking, the climb can be difficult— we recommend you take a city bus to the conveniently located bus stop at the Piazzale. In addition to vendors serving snacks and drinks, there is a nice place to eat. If you have time, look around at the nearby churches before catching the bus. We especially recommend San Miniato Church at the very top of the hill. There is a bus stop in front that will take you back to the train station.

AWESOME SOUVENIRS & GIFTS

If you want to find something nice from Florence, look in the market beside San Lorenzo Church. You will find leather items such as hand bags,  belts and other interesting leather items and locally made goods. Another market closer to the Arno River, called **Mercato Nuovo**, has wonderful buys too. We found some awesome souvenirs in the Oltrarno district. There are a number of artisan shops near the Pitti Palace offering locally crafted souvenirs. We most enjoyed shopping in the Oltrarno area and found unique wood crafted items made in Florence. You can also find nice items from Venice and Murano such as masks and jewelry. If you just want some inexpensive items such as hand held fans (Sydney's favorite) and t-shirts, you can find these throughout the city.

NEAT FOODS

If you like ice cream, **gelato** is one of the most delightful treats to eat in Florence. Gelato is very creamy and flavorful. Since gelato is so well loved, there are many locations offering this delicious treat. Our advice is to try as many as your grown-ups will allow! You will find some most unusual flavors—be brave and try new ones! You can sample flavors before making your choice and deciding, one scoop or two? We recommend not filling up on gelato, since Florence has some great pizza and pasta. Delicious cheese pizzas, called margherita pizza, are in just about every place you might find food and are quite popular.

Sydney Says...
"The margherita pizza
is the best!"

EXTRAS

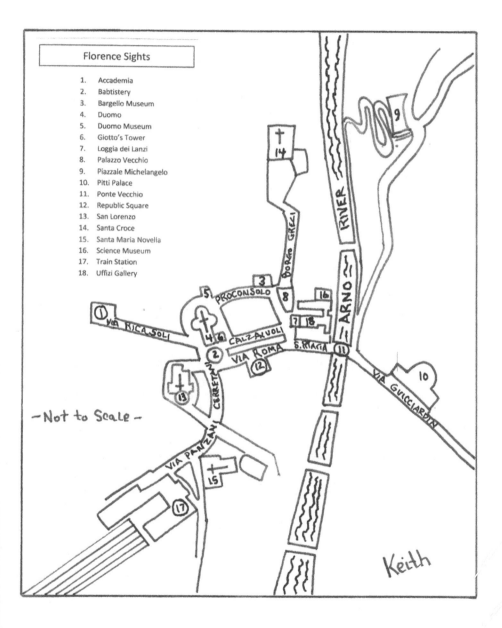

Florence Sights

1. Accademia
2. Babtistery
3. Bargello Museum
4. Duomo
5. Duomo Museum
6. Giotto's Tower
7. Loggia dei Lanzi
8. Palazzo Vecchio
9. Piazzale Michelangelo
10. Pitti Palace
11. Ponte Vecchio
12. Republic Square
13. San Lorenzo
14. Santa Croce
15. Santa Maria Novella
16. Science Museum
17. Train Station
18. Uffizi Gallery

-Not to Scale -

Keith

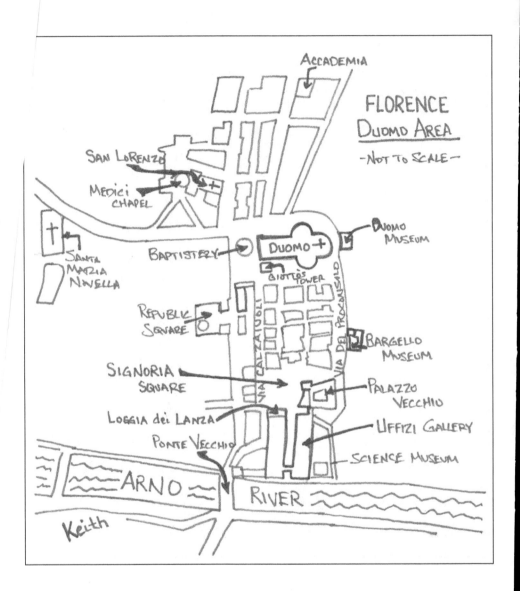

ACCADEMIA

FLORENCE
DUOMO AREA
—NOT TO SCALE—

SAN LORENZO

MEDICI
CHAPEL

DUOMO
MUSEUM

SANTA
MARIA
NOVELLA

BAPTISTERY

DUOMO +

GIOTTO'S
TOWER

VIA DEI PROCONSOLO

REPUBLIC
SQUARE

BARGELLO
MUSEUM

SIGNORIA
SQUARE

VIA CALZAIVOLI

PALAZZO
VECCHIO

LOGGIA dei LANZA

UFFIZI GALLERY

PONTE VECCHIO

SCIENCE MUSEUM

ARNO

RIVER

Keith

Famous Citizens of Florence 1

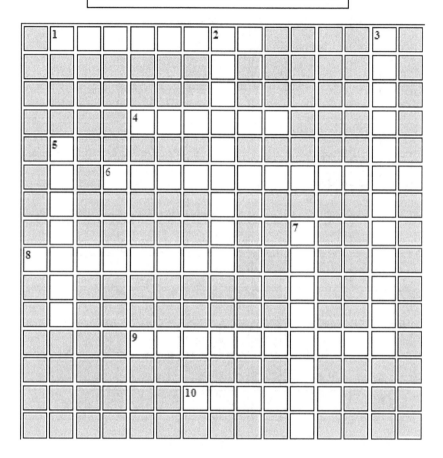

Down

2. Sculpted bronze statue David
3. Created Famous Dome
5. Painted Madonna and Goldfinch
7. Created Baptistery bronze doors

Across

1. "Renaissance man" painted Mona Lisa
4. Painted ceiling of Palazzo Vechhio
6. Sculpted marble statue David
8. Painted The Holy Trinity
9. Painted The Birth of Venus
10. Designed bell tower for Duomo

Check name spelling on the "Renaissance Timeline" page.

Famous Citizens of Florence 2

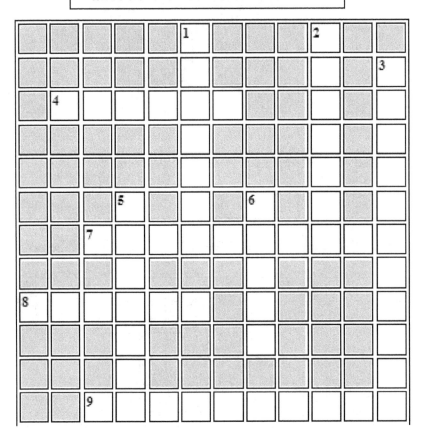

Down

1. Known as "magnificent"
2. New world named after him
3. Wrote The Prince
5. Discovered Jupiter's moons
6. Wrote The Divine Comedy

Across

4. Wrote The Lives of Artists
7. Bonfire of the vanites
8. Wealthy family, patron of arts
9. Tracked comets in night sky

Check name spelling on the "Renaissance Timeline" page.

Florence Word Find 1

```
              R  S
           S  E  G  A
        S  P  A  F  X  X
     D  Q  F  G  O  O  W  X
  L  F  Z  C  P  H  O  C  P  Q
I  A  P  I  Z  Z  A  L  E  A  A  C
U  S  R  D  A  O  D  F  A  S  A  X  T  K
G  F  T  N  S  A  N  L  O  R  E  N  Z  O  R  B
B  T  N  Z  O  V  V  Q  G  X  X  O  A  G  A  T  O  R
K  P  I  T  T  I  P  A  L  A  C  E  U  P  T  H  M  B  N  P
B  H  N  P  O  N  T  E  V  E  C  C  H  I  O  J  X  G  C  W
  A  Q  S  A  N  T  A  C  R  O  C  E  P  M  A  V  F  M
     P  O  Z  D  L  R  V  F  B  A  R  G  E  L  L  O
        T  J  N  P  A  C  C  A  D  E  M  I  A  X
           I  T  M  U  F  F  I  Z  I  X  A  A
              S  D  Y  H  G  M  K  P  R  A
                 T  U  G  U  L  T  Z  N
                    E  O  J  D  P  R
                       R  M  J  F
                          Y  O
```

ARNO	PITTI PALACE
BAPTISTERY	PIZZALE
BARGELLO	PONTE VECCHIO
DUOMO	SAN LORENZO
GUILDS	SANTA CROCE
LOGGIA LANZI	UFFIZI
PATRON	

Florence Word Find 2

```
M R M A C H I A V E L L I R V W
I D K D O N A T E L L O P E E F
C Y G C P E C E T K T V I N R O
H P R E I Q K H L T C L M A R G
E R G L N N B B O Q L Z E I O G
L S H L O R A I W E U C D S C H
A A I I C N G R C D Z J I S C I
N V R N C I L I T C A D C A H B
G O L I H R T E R U A N I N I E
E N A C I T Q G W Z Z T T C O R
L A N D O M F C R A P H A E L T
O R D B R U N E L L E S C H I I
A O A H L E O N A R D O V X D A
I L I S R A V L O R E N Z O H M
B A O W M A S A C C I O T P U P
N E G A L I L E O W F F J X Y W
```

BOTTICELLI   LORENZO
BRUNELLESCHI   MACHIAVELLI
CELLINI   MASACCIO
DANTE   MEDICI
DONATELLO   MICHELANGELO
GALILEO   PINOCCHIO
GHIBERTI   RAPHAEL
GHIRLANDAIO   RENAISSANCE
GIOTTO   SAVONAROLA
LEONARDO   VERROCCHIO

Florence Word Find 3

```
    D H W                           L E D
  R J H M Y Q                   M A R B L E
X E H D H O A C C             Y B A N K I N G Y
S O R U K A B P S             V Q V N B J H C E
T I U R N Q P N S Y         J R E P U B L I C P
S V G E R R P D A S         K E L U C C A Y O I
O W I N M L V T I F B     A F S S L R S A V E S
  S Y I O O E U N E R P F I O T U V D E E O J
    X M T R X S T F O W I E T V S S Q X L P
        X R I C J H N B R S N L K S S
            A O C Z G D O A T
          Q V N H J E M O L I O Z C
        T U D Y N P F T H E V R F P J
      H M W S B B T L L G R Q B K I Z D O Q
    Q P S O B Y M R W O Q X U P P T P O A B A
    S D P O D L N K L R A D W S I I N O B V T
Z V B Q L O I E A M E R C N O C F F V E F I C
L H O V Q R L E O   N N R   Z U A X Z L O W D
L L F C O F Y B I   T O C   N R G N F L A M Z
N J X L N G H M     I R N     H A A S S C V H
D J F L N G O       A I U     E R O M A N S
  E Z C D H         Z V F       C G H Y L
    X D E           V E A       J P I
                    T R W
                    J I S
```

ARNO RIVER	LUCCA
BANKING	MARBLE
BELLS	PISA
BRONZE	REPUBLIC
DAVID	ROMANS
ETRUSCANS	SAINT JOHN
FIESOLE	SIENA
FLORENTIA	SIGNORIA
FLORIN	TUSCANY
LILY	WOOL

Word Match

Draw a line to match what belongs together.

Ponte Vecchio	Baptistery doors
Michelangelo	The Prince
Brunelleschi	"rebirth"
Gates of Paradise	Bargello
St. John	Before the Romans
Florin	David
Galileo	The Duomo
Botticelli	Dante
Notebooks	The Birth of Venus
Old Jail	Gold coin
Renaissance	Telescopes
Uffizi	Leonardo da Vinci
The Divine Comedy	Patron Saint of Florence
Machiavelli	Famous art museum
Etruscans	Old bridge

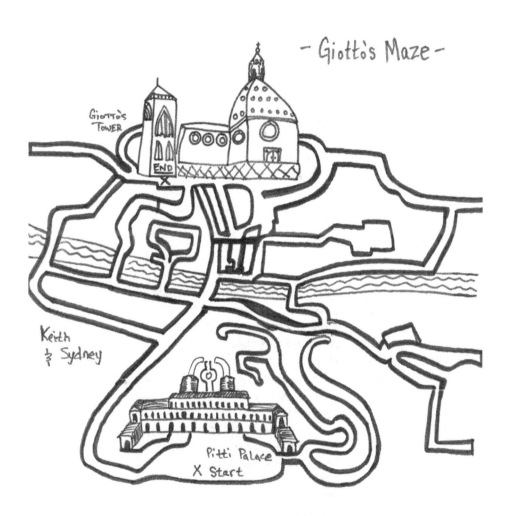

- Giotto's Maze -

Giotto's Tower

END
X

Keith & Sydney

Pitti Palace
X Start

Renaissance Timeline

(Hint: use this to check your spelling in the word find puzzles.)

1265	1321	**Dante**
1267	1337	**Giotto**
1350	1500	"Early" Renaissance
1377	1446	**Brunelleschi**
1378	1455	**Ghiberti**
1386	1466	**Donatello**
1389	1464	**Cosimo de' Medici**
1397	1482	**Paolo Toscanelli**
1401	1428	**Masaccio**
1416		Donatello completes *St. George*
1420		Brunelleschi begins work on the Dome
1427		Masaccio *Holy Trinity of the Matrix*
1435	1488	**Verrocchio**
1436		Brunelleschi completes the Dome
1445	1510	**Botticelli**
1449	1492	**Lorenzo "The Magnificent" Medici**
1452	1519	**Leonardo da Vinci**
1452		Ghiberti completes Baptistery doors
1454	1512	**Amerigo Vespucci**
1469	1527	**Machiavelli**
1475	1564	**Michelangelo**
1480		Botticelli's *The Spring*
1483	1520	**Raphael**
1485		Botticelli's *The Birth of Venus*
1498		Savonarola burned at the stake
1500	1650	"High" Renaissance
1504		Michelangelo completes the *David*
1511	1574	**Vasari**
1564	1642	**Galileo Galilei**
1610		Galileo discovers moons of Jupiter

Sketch Page

Sketch Page

Journal Page

Journal Page

Puzzle Key

Left crossword:

```
1LEONAR 2DO        3B
        O          R
        N          U
     4V A S A R I  N
5R      T          E
A 6M I C H E L A N G E L O
P       L          L
H       L      7G  E
8M A S A C C I O   H    S
E           I      C
L           B      H
     9B O T T I C E L L I
            R
     10G I O T T O
            I
```

Right crossword:

```
            1L           2A
            O        M   3M
    4V A S A R I     E    A
            E        R    C
            N        I    H
       5G   Z    6D  G    I
    7S A V O N A R O L A
       L         N        V
8M E D I C I     T        E
       L         E        L
       E                  L
    9T O S C A N E L L I
```

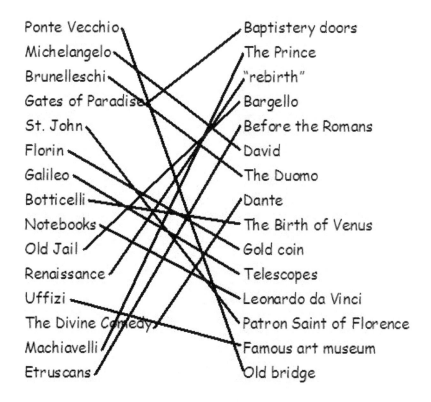

Ponte Vecchio	Baptistery doors
Michelangelo	The Prince
Brunelleschi	"rebirth"
Gates of Paradise	Bargello
St. John	Before the Romans
Florin	David
Galileo	The Duomo
Botticelli	Dante
Notebooks	The Birth of Venus
Old Jail	Gold coin
Renaissance	Telescopes
Uffizi	Leonardo da Vinci
The Divine Comedy	Patron Saint of Florence
Machiavelli	Famous art museum
Etruscans	Old bridge

CPSIA information can be obtained
at www.ICGtesting.com
Printed in the USA
BVHW07s2156250618
519781BV00008B/234/P